BORN

THE SECRET

IN

DAUGHTER'S

ADULTERY

MEMOIR

Tamara!
It's a blessing to have
a high school

HEATHER JAMES MILLER

Scripture quotations marked (NLT) are taken from the Holy Bible, New Living Translation, copyright © 1996, 2004, 2007, 2013, 2015 by Tyndale House Foundation. Used by permission of Tyndale House Publishers, Inc., Carol Stream, Illinois 60188. All rights reserved.

Scripture taken from the New King James Version®. Copyright © 1982 by Thomas Nelson. Used by permission. All rights reserved.

Scripture quotations marked (NLT) are taken from the Holy Bible, New Living Translation, copyright © 1996, 2004, 2007, 2013, 2015 by Tyndale House Foundation. Used by permission of Tyndale House Publishers, Inc., Carol Stream, Illinois 60188. All rights reserved.
Scripture quotations marked (NIV) are taken from the Holy Bible, New International Version®, NIV®. Copyright © 1973, 1978, 1984, 2011 by Biblica, Inc.® Used by permission of Zondervan. All rights reserved worldwide. www.zondervan.com The "NIV" and "New International Version" are trademarks registered in the United States Patent and Trademark Office by Biblica, Inc.®

Cover Design: Heather James Miller, LLC
Front & Back Cover Image/Photographer: Erick Robinson Photography
Interior Design: Heather James Miller, LLC.
Copy Editor: Beth Kallman Werner, Author Connections
Editor: Janiah Sanford Black Lily Content Management Group Janiah Sanford
Publish Services: Heather James Miller, LLC

Library of Congress Cataloging-in-Publication data
ISBN: 978-0-578-87642-9
First Edition

Printed in the United States of America

To Barbara, the angel that helped me heal.

CONTENTS

ACKNOWLEDGMENTS

Ronney, Devin, Malachi, and Genesis, your patience, kindness, and understanding while I birthed this project is evidence of your genuine love.

Grandma, thanks for making me write when I didn't want to, I'm an author now just like you.

Danielle, my sister, your confidence in me is a gift I'll treasure forever.

Carla and Sam thank you for being my prayer warriors, secret keepers, and cheerleaders through every part of this project.

Mom, your love is rare. Thank you for the sacrifices you made throughout my life. Not only have I noticed them, but I also lost track of trying to count them. I'm the woman I am today because you taught me that it's okay to color outside the lines.

Daddy, I'm able to forgive without limits and give without expecting anything in return because of you. Dinner at Eight by Pottery Barn will forever be our album, and you will forever be in my heart. Rest In Peace.

To my dear friends and family members unmentioned, know that your love and support has not gone unnoticed.

CHAPTER ONE

Some of my favorite childhood memories were spending time at my grandmother Freshy's house. The ride to Marshall Street seemed to take forever, coming off the Ben Franklin Bridge into North Philadelphia. During the times I spent in Philly, every day was action-packed, unlike the quiet neighborhood where we lived just thirty minutes south in New Jersey.

Every time we drove through the narrow Philadelphia streets clustered with potholes, my mother would point out a small home doctor's office where she used to take my sister and me when we were little, slowing down just enough so I'd observe and appreciate how much our lives had changed since moving across the state line. She'd ask me if I remembered living on N. 6th Street in the apartment building Freshy owned. I always said I remembered.

As my mother turned the corner onto N. Marshall Street, I'd stick my head out the window as we got closer to Freshy's house, so I could see if any of my friends were playing outside. Freshy's good friends had grandchildren my age who also came to visit every summer. They were the only kids I could play with.

Hanging my head out the window to feel the summer breeze against my face was a given. It was the best way to see people sitting out on their stoops, listening to loud music on boomboxes, cracking sunflower seeds, and drinking quarter waters while singing loudly to the music that echoed from West Berks to West Norris streets. Teenage boys playing handball as a stream of water rushed alongside the curb, carrying street litter. This meant one thing—the fire hydrant was on and some lucky kid had their backside positioned over the opening to create a waterfall. Every year, the block came together and chipped in to buy colorful flags to hang from the second-floor window of each house. It was a vivid distraction from old sneakers hanging on the power lines.

I could always tell Freshy was super excited to see me. She was my father's mother, and we looked so much alike, judging by the glow in her eyes, she saw in me a younger version of herself. Freshy always had a surprise for me, too. She'd send me to go fetch it while she and my mother sat on the stoop, chatting. My mother said when we lived around the corner in Freshy's apartment building, Freshy used to give me gifts all the time. She babysat me while my mother went to work, up until we moved.

Freshy was a large woman; about six feet tall, thick in the middle, with fleshy arms and a bosom that would swallow your entire head when she gave you a hug. Her skin was smooth and soft, like buttery leather, the perfect shade of mahogany. She had silky, dyed-burgundy hair that she somehow kept in a bun on top of her head with just one bobby pin.

One particular visit to Freshy's was different than the rest. As we pulled up behind her sparkling clean green coupe Deville with leather seats, she was sitting on the marble stoop. It was easy to spot her blushing face as she stood with her hands on her hips to greet me.

Freshy's house was tiny, so the moment you opened the screen door you could smell the aroma of seasoned fried chicken, buttered yeast rolls, and vanilla cake that I nicknamed 'clean cake'. In the narrow foyer stood a stained oak coat rack combination with a centered mirror and bench, and adjacent was the parlor room with a white contemporary velour sofa covered in plastic. The sofa held an array of ruffled dresses from the Puerto Rican shops on Broad Street, skort sets (a combination of a skirt and shorts that was loose and flowy enough that you could barely tell the difference), short sets, separates, underdress slips, camisoles, and several packs of cotton panties from Strawbridge and Clothier in downtown Center City. She also had a box of brand new patent leather Mary-Jane shoes from the Italians in South Philly, large ruffle socks from the corner bodega, and a half-full brown bag of my favorite penny candies. Freshy did this every time I came to stay with her. I never needed to pack a bag when visiting her, she'd buy me everything I needed for several weeks.

Freshy yelled from the front step, "You find everything, babe?"
I yelled back with excitement, "I found it!" Then, I questioned, "Freshy, you make a cake?"
 "Get on out my kitchen and come show your mother your things."
I never could figure out how she knew where I was in that house, but I was definitely in the kitchen, opening pot lids.

I carried everything to the stoop outside, showing my mother my new dresses, matching outfits, shoes, and lace-ruffled socks. I didn't show her my candy, because she would fuss about my teeth. As I hugged Freshy to say thank you, my mother commented with a smile, "Ree, you spoil her."
Freshy admitted, "That's my baby."

Saying goodbye to my mother for a while made me sad, but I had more friends and things to get into at Freshy's than I did at home. I was a momma's girl, so ultimately, I was only going to miss being up underneath her. Once my mother drove off, Freshy yelled to the kids playing under the hydrant water, "Get out the street!" Her voice was bold and loud; it could be heard for at least three blocks. Sitting on the stoop, people-watching was my favorite thing to do with Freshy. She had all the scoop on everyone on the block. She knew just what to tell me, and then she'd say, "Don't repeat that, you hear me?"

As the day grew later, her friends walked down the block to see me and make small talk, just before buying a pint of Freshy's homemade moonshine. My grandmother was from Georgia. Her parents had moved up north and opened businesses—very successful businesses. They owned a restaurant, a dry-cleaning service, several apartment buildings, and a beauty parlor. There was a constant flow of people coming to the house, wanting to buy everything from a plate of food or a pound of produce to a homemade cake, a bottle of beer, and of course her famous moonshine.

They all knew better than to ask me to run and get anything. One time, a guy who lived a few houses down—"Mister C"—asked me to fetch him a beer from the kitchen. I ran in the kitchen, excited to be playing store, I put the money in Freshy's apron as she was standing cooking over the stove. As I was grabbing a beer and a brown bag, she said, "What do you think you are doing, Freshpot?!" (That's what she called me.)

"Mister C ordered a beer," I answered. She snatched that beer out my hand so quick, I didn't even notice it was gone. Then, she walked to the front door so fast I thought she was going to warp straight through it. By the time I caught up, she had laid into Mister C so good that he gave me ten dollars and an apology.

As Freshy walked back in the house, she was mumbling, "Don't ask my baby to get you no beer, who you think you are…" Mister C looked at me and said, "I don't know why your grandmother gets so bent out of shape."

She yelled from inside, "And get off my stoop if you gonna talk about me!" Mister C and I laughed.

Freshy had a tenant who lived in her house. Mister David was his name; he was a truck driver. He babbled a lot when he talked—all his words ran together. I got a dollar every time he saw me. Freshy would allow Mister David to eat dinner with us. He had to pay, though, right before grace.

Dinner was served at five o'clock on the dot. It felt more like a late lunch, so by the time the streetlights came on, I was hungry again. After dinner, I had to get washed up and ready for bed. Freshy said, "If you eat too late, you'll have nightmares." I knew better than to debate with her, so I'd eat a few pieces of candy out my brown bag while sitting naked on the edge of the tub as it filled with water.

I had my own room, but I was too scared to sleep by myself. There were two doors, one that led to Freshy's bedroom and the other to the hallway; that door remained locked with a bolt. Plus, the 13" color TV was in her room. I'd put my nightdress on, walk into her room, climb into her white crisp sheets, and rest my head on two of the four feather pillows on the bed, as if I had no other option. She never said anything.

Early in the summer, on Thursday nights we'd watch Jeopardy, Wheel of Fortune, Family Ties, and any show but The Cosby Show. To say Freshy hated Bill Cosby was an understatement. If you mentioned him or his show, she'd tell you how ridiculous he was, followed by, "You don't know him, and you not watching him in my house." I said to myself, *You don't know Pat or Vanna, but we watch them every night.* I wanted to keep my lips, so I kept them sealed and said nothing out loud.

In all the years I spent with her, Freshy spanked me one time. We took a bus trip to Disney World with everyone on the block, and I wanted to hang with the forbidden kids. She told me no, and I huffed and puffed, then stomped into our hotel room bathroom and slammed the door. When I came out, she had a flip flop in her hand and demanded that I come to her. I never knew rubber could hurt so bad. I never tried her again.

When it came to Cosby, I just figured by her owning a restaurant and cooking for a lot of people, maybe she and Cosby's paths had crossed, or maybe she knew something then that other people only know now. All I know for certain is she didn't like him, and I could not watch that show in her house.

Freshy had arthritis in her knees, and every night she'd sit on the edge of the bed, rubbing green alcohol on them and wrapping them with an ace bandage. Once she finished this routine, the whole room smelled like a medical facility.

Later in the summer, when there wasn't much on TV, she'd reach for her pack of playing cards that were held together by a red rubber band on top of her king-size bookcase headboard. Solitaire was her nighttime game of choice. After she won a few times, the lights went out and in the window she went. If it wasn't too busy outside, I could sit on her lap. There was a chair that sat right up to the window; it was her favorite spot. She'd lean over just far enough to look up and down the block. And yes, she would yell out the window. Freshy was in everyone's business. Everyone on the block respected her; they knew better than to talk back.

When the streets calmed down and got quiet, it was time to go to bed. I'd start praying, asking God to protect us during the night, for the Lord to cover my mother, my sister, and to help my father quit smoking. Freshy would whisper goodnight and tell me to get under all the sheets and move over. After I heard her snoring for a bit, I'd crawl up under her and wrap my arm around her neck real tight.

Saturday mornings were anticipated because that's when all the good cartoons came on. It's also when the random produce guy would come chanting from his megaphone, driving two miles an hour down the street. "I gotcha mean green beans and tomatoes for soup; I gotcha peaches, apples, oranges to eat on your stoop; come on out and get your fresh-produce!" Only a few people would make it out to the street in time. Freshy wasn't one of them, so she'd yell up the stairs for me to put my housecoat on and run outside to stop the truck. By the time he pulled up, she was halfway out of the house yelling what she wanted. Cash in hand and ready to strike a deal, she came down the steps telling him she wasn't about to be playing "the price is right" with him.

Freshy was bossy and funny; people seemed to like it. One Saturday, after she had the guy take her purchase inside the house, Freshy told me to go get dressed. As I was putting on my shoes, I heard the phone ring. I could hear her yelling, but couldn't make out what she was saying. Someone had her livid. When I came downstairs, I looked in the hallway cabinet like I always did, at my father's daughter's college photo. I didn't know much about her, except that she was really smart and graduated from a famous Ivy League school.

When I walked into the kitchen, Freshy looked disturbed. It was my first time ever seeing her look truly concerned. She told me that after breakfast I needed to go over to her friend's house a few doors down, to hurry up and eat. She said that she had to run some errands.

Something felt off. Freshy would never leave me over someone's house. I always had to stay in her sight.

After I ate my breakfast with coffee, she told me to mind my manners and she would come to get me when she returned. As I proceeded toward the front of the house, she yelled, "Wait!" I stopped. She slammed her hand on the table, mumbling and talking to herself. She then yelled, hesitantly, "Go ahead, and hurry." She yelled louder, "Runnn!"

I quickly ran out of the house. Freshy's friend's granddaughter was waiting outside. She said, "Let's go in the house and play with my Barbies." I was excited to play with the Barbies, but I was worried about Freshy. What felt like hours went by and from what I could tell, Freshy's car never left from in front of the house. I had a feeling that something awful was going to happen.

It got cloudy outside and thunder could be heard from a distance. Moments later, I looked back out the doorway and it was pouring rain. I noticed a red car pulled up to Freshy's house. Just as a woman's arm extended from the front driver's seat to open her umbrella, Freshy's friend yelled, "Heather, get from in front of that door." I backed up and ran to the sofa. Freshy's other friend was there in the kitchen, sitting at the table, drinking coffee and smoking a Virginia Slim. I could hear her whisper, "Why is Heather here?" and then a muffled response, "Her daughter-in law is coming over; she needed to hide Heather until she leaves." I kept staring at the television as if I heard nothing.

* * * * *

My mother told me at a very early age that my father had another family: a wife and two kids, a daughter and a son. She explained that just because he had another family did not mean that I was loved any less or would be treated differently. She assured me that she and my father would do anything for me, because they loved and adored me.

I recall asking one time about when I would go to meet my siblings, and she responded, "It's complicated, because they don't know you exist."
"So, is my dad going to tell them about me, so I can meet them?"
"Not right now!"
"When?"

She explained that she and my father were once in a

forbidden relationship, before I was born. She affirmed that I was a gift from God. She added, "If his wife or children found out about you, they would be hurt and might not understand."

Every so often during the years of my youth, I asked the same question. "When is my dad going to tell his other family about me?" Each time, my mother gave the same answer: "Not right now!" It became obvious to me that I was unequivocally a mystery and needed to remain that way.

My father was around quite often when I was small. My earliest recollection is from when I was three or four years old. My mother finds it bizarre that I remember details from that age. We lived in Freshy's apartment building in North Philadelphia. It was a nice size—not too big, not too small. The building was on a busy one-way street. From the steps, looking at the brick building—four stories up—was intimidating; the double doors that led into the foyer held six mailboxes built into the wall. There was no elevator; just winding steps with a wide wooden banister. Each floor had a dim fixture offering just enough light to see and get your key inside the lock.

Our place was said to be the best unit in the building. The walls were painted emerald green, and when you walked in on the hardwood floors, you entered the center of the living room. Straight ahead, we had a blue velour sofa that was pushed up against the wall, centered directly under a narrow window with ivory-colored, chipped paint. The kitchen was to the right, and to the left, one step up from the living room was a short hallway that led to my parents' room. Another hallway led to the bedroom my sister and I shared.

Every night before bed, in the early mornings, and half the day on Sundays, my father was with us—me, my sister, and my mother. I can recall many nights of dancing in the living room, jazz records playing while my sister and I hopped around as if we were ballerinas in a show. I also remember being tucked in at night, then getting out of bed to jump in bed with my mother and father. A red box of chocolate-covered cherry cordials was often on the dresser. In the summer, the smell of sweet cherry cordials covered in milk chocolate permeated the room.

I remember the day we moved out, when someone took my broken baby stroller and threw it over a fence. After moving to another area of Pennsylvania, I didn't see my father as much. We took family trips to Disney World; Williamsburg, Virginia; and Georgia, to visit his cousins. They made a huge fuss over seeing me every year. Once we moved to New Jersey, though, I only saw my father after dinner on Sundays.

When I was visiting Freshy in Philadelphia, I got to see him much more. Spending time with Freshy and my father together meant lots of laughs. She was no-nonsense, and most people humbled themselves in her presence. Not my father, though; he'd go toe to toe with her. She'd send him out to get empty bottles for her speak-easy and he'd say, "Mom, you shouldn't be doing that!" His refusal often resulted in her cussing him out. Freshy could cuss, too— every syllable could be heard and felt, giving the word even more emphasis.

* * * * *

On the day that Freshy hid me over at her friend's house while her daughter in law came to visit, it wasn't long after overhearing her friends talking in the kitchen that Freshy called and gave instructions for me to come back. I ran out that house so fast, through the rain, and as soon as I ran up the steps, Freshy was waiting in the doorway. I gave her a huge hug and she hugged me back, real tight. That hug said so much it made me cry. She asked me if I was okay, and I told her I missed her. She said, "I missed you too." We went into the dining room and spent the rest of the day peeling peas out of the pod, watching TV.

There was the silence of guilt between us. She knew she hid me, and I knew she never left.

I was too afraid to tell Freshy what I'd overheard. I knew she loved me, a lot. Now, looking back, I know she didn't want to hide me, but I look a great deal like her and my father. She was an only child, so I wasn't a niece or nephew. Her oldest son died not long before I was born, and he didn't have any children. There was no way to explain who I was. Her revealing who I was could have meant severing the relationship with her only living son and possibly never seeing me again.

* * * * *

Six or seven-years later, we went to visit Freshy after church. When she came to open the front door, she didn't have her usual excitement to see me. Something was off. Freshy was not excited this day. It was odd that she wasn't sitting on the front porch, and it was odd that the lights were off. There was no aroma of food at all. It appeared that before we arrived, she had been sitting in the dark.

My mother had to tell Freshy who we were before she would open the door. She said she knew, but she showed no expression. When she invited us in, albeit hesitantly, she had us sit in her front parlor as if she was entertaining strangers. Her conversation with us was vague and it seemed as if she had little interest in us being there. While we were sitting, she started petting the air in front of her as if it was an animal in her lap. She said, "Look at my little puppy, ain't he the cutest puppy you've ever seen?"

I looked at my mother for her reaction, because I was scared! I asked my mother what was wrong, and she said, "Your grandmother's memory is leaving her. It appears she has an early onset of Alzheimer's disease."

When my mother got up and went into the kitchen, she found it in shambles. She immediately started cleaning up. My mother could clean a house in under a minute. She was fast and thorough, supremely efficient. She loved Freshy as much as I did. Freshy had been good to her over the years, rented to her for free and babysat me for no charge. After scrubbing the kitchen and dining area, my mother found an open jar of half-eaten peaches just lying on the floor. Freshy would have never eaten straight from a jar, let alone have food of any kind on the floor.

Afterward, we walked her upstairs, washed her up from the basin bowl, and I plaited her hair. As we sat on the edge of the bed, I started asking her questions as I brushed her soft ombre burgundy and black hair. I asked who her mother and father were, and surprisingly, she answered and went on and on about them. I grabbed a pen and piece of paper and started writing it all down. Questions I didn't think to ask years prior, I started asking. If her memory was leaving her, I needed to know as much as possible about my family.

We waited until she was in bed, sleep and for Mister David to get home, before we left to go home. On the way back home to New Jersey, my mother explained to me the severity of Alzheimer's disease. I was heartbroken. She said she would go over in the morning before going to work, to call my father at work and let him know he needed to get over there and take her home with him immediately. I responded to call him right away, not to wait. She said she could only reach him at work.

My mother said there was a chance I'd never see Freshy again. "Why?!!" I asked. She said, "Soon, Freshy will no longer be able to live by herself, she needs to be looked after. She's going to need to live with your dad's family, and since things are complicated, you won't be able to go over there to see her." I was crushed, deeply gutted. It felt like I had just lost my best friend. I sobbed and cried.

Little did I know, it was only the beginning of a journey filled with more pain. I needed God to heal my heart more than ever.

I knew of God at an early age. As a child, I went to Catholic church just about every Sunday, and when I got home, I was disciplined for acting up. I was extremely loud and restless. I hated church and dreaded going. When we switched over to a Pentecostal church, I don't recall getting in trouble as much. It was too upbeat and entertaining to fall asleep. I really enjoyed singing in the choir. I can recall moments when I even got emotional if the song pertained to something I was going through.

The older I got, the more I understood who God was, and what it meant having Him in my life. I grew to love going to church. I had friends there, mentors there; one helped to groom me as a young lady of elegance, another made exceptions for me due to my learning disability. I learned scriptures at vacation bible school and how to understand the bible at Bible Study.

Having a foundation in God taught me that there is a higher-power watching over my life, no weapon formed against me will never prosper, and the plan for my life involved prospering. I learned to pray to the Lord for all things that concern my heart, because what concerned me, concerned GOD! In the morning on the way to school, in the car before going somewhere, and in bed before going to sleep at night, my mother had me pray. To sum up my prayers as a kid, it was all about my father; for him to stop smoking and to tell his family about me so that I could see him all the time and meet my brother and sister.

CHAPTER TWO

Every year, my father would take me clothes shopping just before school started. One summer, he kept canceling. Something kept coming up. So, we ended up going shopping after the school year started.

He picked me up from my mother's house, and we traveled up to Fort Dix military base to shop since he was retired from the Air Force. Designer clothes and shoes were less expensive on the base. Shortly after arriving, we headed into the PX and he said—rather anxiously—that he needed to get a haircut. He told me to go ahead and get what I needed. Like every other time we went shopping, prices never mattered and there was no budget, so it wasn't unusual for him to leave me to get what I wanted, but this time he was distracted by something.

After I filled the cart with clothes, shoes, and school supplies, I didn't see him in the front of the store, where he'd promised to be waiting. I circled the store, then came back to the front, but still he wasn't there. Finally, I decided to stay still and just wait. I don't recall how long I waited, but it felt like a long time. When he finally popped back in, he rushed me to the front of the checkout line, telling a customer waiting in line that he'd appreciate it if they would let us go first. The lady never got a chance to respond.

After quickly paying for everything, he said we had to go. Normally, we'd grab lunch a few stores down, but this time we had to leave right away. As we were leaving, I heard a man calling my father's name. My father's name is rare, so it was certain this man was calling for him and desired his attention. After the guy's shout grew closer, my father, visibly annoyed, stopped. I could sense he was irritated.

The guy jogged up to us, out of breath. They greeted each other, and the man said, "I saw you when you first got here, how are you?" His eyes shifted toward me and before my father could respond, the man inquisitively asked who I was. Hesitant to respond, my father said, "Oh this is Heather." I reached my hand out to shake the man's hand and as he shook my hand, my father abruptly grabbed me and we started walking off.

Now even more curious, the man followed my father and asked, "Heather who?" He appeared confused and wanted an explanation, "oh this is Heather" didn't satisfy his curiosity. My father avoided the question and said, "Heather go on and get in the car." As I started walking, I could hear my father whispering but I couldn't make out what he said. When he got into the car it was quiet. My bubble had burst, and I was now living in reality. I had never been introduced as 'Heather' before. Even at my his job, my father's co-workers knew me as his daughter. Why was it different with this guy?

My feelings were crushed. It was a silent ride back home. When he dropped me off, he pulled a couple hundred dollars out of his wallet and apologized for rushing our time together. He walked in to tell my mother he had to run. He hugged and kissed me like always, but this time even bags filled with clothes and a couple hundred dollars wasn't going to fix my broken heart.

When my mother asked me if I was okay, I told her what happened, but she made it out to be nothing. My mother is one of those people who sees the good in EVERYTHING. She made up scenarios and excuses for my father, questioning if I actually saw and heard what I know I saw and heard. The more she questioned, the more furious I became. I needed her to be on my side, I wanted her to be pissed off at him with me. I needed her to see that my father had just denied that I was his daughter.

All I could think about was telling my boyfriend. He was one of the few people I could talk to who would understand, because he had issues with his own father. I tried calling him several times and got no answer. By the time I got in touch with him, he had news of his own to tell me—he no longer wanted to be my boyfriend. He broke up with me. Rejection on top of rejection hit me like a ton of bricks. It was as if a film of my life was playing in my head, from hiding from my father's wife on that rainy day at my grandma's, to a breakup from a boyfriend, and finally, my father introducing me as 'Heather'. I couldn't help but question, *What did he whisper to that man? What couldn't he say in front of me?* People only whisper about secrets. I was a secret holding on to secrets, from being molested by a family member, to who I was and who I belonged to. It was too much for me.

I cried out to God and it felt like His presence was nowhere near. My foundation in Christ felt shattered. I had questions: Why did you allow all this to happen to me? Why didn't you protect me? The same questions I cried when I couldn't get rid of the torment of being pushed in the closet, in the dark, molested and then threatened to not tell.

With great effort to escape the thoughts in my head, I decided to give in. That night after everyone went to bed, I took an entire bottle of aspirin. I crawled under my sheets and cried as I waited with anticipation for God to take my life. My mother came into my room and asked me if I was okay. I didn't answer her. She sat on the edge of my bed and started praying for me, asking God to give me strength and to show me that better days were on the other side of the pain I was feeling. When she closed out the prayer, I told her I had taken a bottle of pills. I told her I didn't want to live, it might be too late, and to pray I go to heaven. She immediately pushed me out of bed and shoved me into her car.

On our way to the emergency room, she was praying and pleading with God to save my life. I remember feeling extremely fatigued. When we arrived at the hospital, they immediately took me to the back, laid me on the bed, and put a tube in my nose that went to my stomach. It hurt like hell.

After all the aspirins were pumped from my stomach, they kept me for observation before transferring me to another nearby hospital. I could see the disappointment and concern in my mother's eyes. The room in the second hospital didn't look like a normal hospital room. My door was locked. A hospital bed was pushed up against a wall. There was a small window above the bed that was closer to the ceiling than the floor. These doctors weren't wearing white coats with stethoscopes; they were psychologists and therapists. They rotated in and out of the room, each leading with the same question: "Why did you want to take your life?" I didn't have an answer, other than I simply didn't want to live anymore. I didn't want to talk. I wanted to be left alone.

After several hours passed, another doctor came into the room with my mother and father behind her. They sat down in chairs that scuffed the floor when moved, making a loud noise that echoed in the bare room. When the doctor asked why I wanted to take my life, I started to cry. I mumbled the first thought that came to mind that could be fixed, "Because my father didn't tell the guy in the parking lot I was his daughter, and his family still doesn't know that I exist." I ended up blurting out everything that was bothering me.

In our house we didn't discuss pain, we didn't elaborate at length what pain we were feeling on the inside. My mom believed in forgiveness. If someone wronged you, you forgive him or her and move on. That's what she was taught to do. I was different. I could forgive, but naturally everything that was troubling me needed to be addressed.

My mother and father looked as if they were seeing a ghost. They had no idea I had been holding on to so much. My father apologized profusely, and promised to put forth an effort to make things right. He would tell his wife about me. He promised that everything was going to be alright. My mother expressed her love for me and willingness to do whatever it took to make sure I was okay.

After another night of rest and all the right answers to their million questions, I was released from the hospital. I had to attend outpatient therapy and weekly sessions with my high school guidance counselor. They summed up my incident as a cry for help.

* * * * *

Two more years went by, and my father didn't make any progress on his promise. I stopped going to therapy. I was no longer going to the same church, and God felt more like a figment of my imagination than the author of my life.

CHAPTER THREE

When I was a child, my mother's mother, the grandma who lived with us, often made me read the newspaper and write about what I read. I did this just about every other week, and I hated it. It felt like a punishment. If I ever said I was bored or if I was watching TV for too long, she'd grab a book and tell me to read it to her.

One day, the gift of storytelling caught up with me and was used to reach America's most successful black television host, Oprah Winfrey. It was time I took matters into my own hands. I wasn't going to take my life after realizing there was hope. Who better to fix what I was going through? So, after school one day, while my grandma was watching The Oprah Winfrey Show, I noticed in the credits a P.O. Box to send a letter, to be featured on her show.

It took me two days to jot that address down—we didn't have the Pause feature on our television, or the internet, and to dial 411 for information cost about \$.35 too much.

In computer class, I wrote a letter to Harpo Studios and addressed it to Oprah herself. I explained that my father's wife didn't know about me and I wanted to meet her and my siblings. I can't recall how much time passed, but I remember the day her producers called and left a message. It was during Christmas break and I felt like it was a gift from heaven that out of all the letters they received, they called me back!! I must have listened to that voicemail a hundred times.

As I anxiously waited for the weekend to pass so I could return their call, it seemed like an eternity. The minute I got home from school that Monday, I called the producer back. He wanted to know if I was still interested in coming on the show and if my father, his wife, and their kids would come to the show, and tell our story. I said, "YES!" with so much excitement. He wanted to speak to my father, so I gave him his work number.

As I waited with bated breath, I kept picking up the phone to make sure it worked, pacing my mother's room, on edge. Then the phone rang. It was my father. He asked me why I reached out to the people on the Oprah show. I told him I was tired of being a secret. I wanted to meet my family. He said, "Babe, we can't go on national television and tell our business."

"Why not?" He laughed nervously as I said, "This way you don't have to tell your wife, Oprah can tell her. She's skilled for stuff like this."

"No, babe, it doesn't work like that. Let me make some phone calls and I'll get back with you."

Make some phone calls, I thought. Oprah wants to meet us! Who's going to fix this better than Oprah? He called me back almost immediately and said, "You wanna meet your sister?"

I responded emphatically, "Yes!"

"How about Freshy, too? Want to see her too?"

"Absolutely."

"Your sister is on her way, and I'll make sure provisions are made so you can see Freshy."

I was excited. Not as excited as I was to be on The Oprah Winfrey Show, but meeting my sister was a move in the right direction. It gave me more hope.

I don't know why I was nervous, but I was, perhaps it was the jealousy I felt over the years, she had my father in her home and I didn't. I did my hair, changed out of my school clothes, and all I could think about was how I was gaining a sister and finally one step closer to no longer being a secret. Before my mind could race a minute longer, I heard the doorbell ring. The girl in the graduation picture in Freshy's hallway cabinet was at my door in the flesh. My sister! This was all coming together as I had always prayed. My heart leapt into my throat. It was actually happening.

My maternal grandma shouted, "Heather, she's here!" As my grandma opened the door, in walked a more mature young woman than the photo at Freshy's. She appeared to be bi-racial. She was holding her two-year-old daughter. I had heard so much about this child that loved getting into my father's briefcase and decorating it with stickers. She was adorable. I was thinking, *this is my niece. I have a niece!*

When we sat down on the sofa, she asked me a ton of questions about myself. It seemed as if she had literally just found out about me and was here only to help my father, our father, by satisfying my urge to be revealed. It was odd hearing someone else refer to my father as "our daddy". My excitement depleted and I began to feel defensive. I showed her pictures of our father and me from when I was little. Her expressions made it clear that she was learning this news for the first time. I could sense she was uncomfortable but trying to save face.

After about an hour, she stated she had to go before traffic got busy. My father called as she was leaving and asked her to tell me to come to the phone when they were finished talking. She called me over and said, "Daddy wants to talk to you." She gave me a hug and said it was nice to meet me. My father asked me if I was happy, and at that very moment I was. I was content. But the overall experience was a band-aid.

When my mother got home from work, I couldn't wait to share with her everything that had happened. She said she knew that my father would turn down going on the Oprah show, but she hadn't wanted to upset me because I was so excited. I then asked her if my father's wife was white. She said, "No! Why?" I told her that it appeared that his daughter, my half-sister, was bi-racial.

My mother told me that evening that my father and his wife never had a child together. It was her understanding that they were unable to conceive. They adopted my sister, and my father's son, my brother, was conceived before my father was married. She wanted me to understand how my existence could hurt. I didn't care. It was almost as if everyone was protecting my father's wife's feelings over mine. I didn't understand it. Selfish, self-centered, spoiled—call me everything but a child of God, I didn't care. I hated being kept in the dark.

It wasn't long after meeting my sister the first time that my father purchased a car for my birthday. I was able to drive myself and go see Freshy any time I wanted. I only had to call my father first.

Freshy was in a nursing home right up the street from my father's job. I went to see her after school and on weekends. By the time I was in college I had a baby boy, and I would take him to see her as well. When I first started visiting, she was coherent for a little while and then she'd drift off and start talking to me as if I was someone else. She enjoyed seeing my son, Devin, and playing with his baby feet, making him laugh. Those moments didn't last. I treasured them every time they arrived.

It wasn't long before Freshy's health declined. Her foot was amputated, then her leg. Shortly after, she lost her memory for good. Even though it was painful to see her in that condition, I kept going back, just to brush her hair and give her a hug. She may not have known who I was anymore, but I knew exactly who she was to me.

Two days before my birthday, I received a note on

my dorm room door that said, "Meet your dad at your mother's house when you get this. It's important." My mother, stepfather, and grandma cared for Devin while I was at school, so I immediately thought it had to do with him. I tried calling my mother's house phone from the dorm's hallway payphone, but no answer. I tried calling my father's job. No answer. I dropped everything and drove home.

By the time I arrived, my father was already parked in the driveway. I didn't have a clue what he had to tell me, but it must have been serious for him to take off work and ask me to drive over an hour home from school. When I walked into my mother's house it was unusually dim. I could see my mother holding Devin on her hip in the kitchen, and my father was drinking a cup of coffee, sitting on the floral sofa. He asked me to come over and take a seat next to him.

I wanted to grab Devin from my mother, but my father looked grave. The suspense was building and by the look on his face, this was serious. He had a hard time putting his thoughts together. I had never seen my father search for words. He paused, grabbed my hand, tilted his head to the side, and said, "Babe...Ma died." Immediately, my eyes filled with tears to the brim. My heart was shattered. Even though she had mentally left years ago, this was an end to our relationship.

My father held me until I stopped crying and I asked him about the funeral arrangements. He said there would not be a funeral, just a viewing. I asked him would I be able to go. He said he had to work things out, but he would see to it that I could say my final goodbye.

I got up and went into the kitchen, lifted Devin out of his highchair and held him in my arms, crying even more. My mother went into the front living room and sat next to my father on the sofa. They were whispering. Then I heard my mother get agitated, her tone shifted, and she said something like, "That girl needs to say goodbye to her grandmother. She needs closure!" It got quiet, then my mother whispered, "You are such a coward!"

I could hear my father getting upset, his tone turned husky as he got up. He walked into the kitchen and said, "Babe I'm leaving, come give me a hug." I gave him a hug and he left without saying anything else to my mother. I never heard them argue or have a disagreement. Ever. It felt good to hear my mother advocate for me. I asked her if she was okay as she walked into the kitchen, and she responded, "I'm fine, everything is fine." It was obvious she was upset.

There was no way my father would not allow me to see my Freshy. Just as I anticipated, a few days later, my father called to let me know of the date for the viewing. I knew this was horrible timing to meet my brother and his wife and see my sister again. I thought it was God's way of finally bringing the truth to light.

The viewing was on a Friday. Traveling from college I got caught up in traffic and it took me almost two hours. When I arrived at the funeral home, the doors were locked. I knocked profusely, tapped on windows, but no one answered. I walked around the back of the building and hopped through the high grass—that needed grooming—to bang on the back door. Just before I could get to the steps, a guy came out and asked if he could help me. I mentioned that I was late for the viewing, and gave him Freshy's real name. He said that they were closed and the director had gone home for the day. He apologized that he couldn't help me, but everything was locked up.

I kept saying "Oh no, oh no, oh no," in disappointment. He said, "Don't worry, if you come early Monday before the funeral, you can see her then. Stay right here, let me go see exactly what time it starts."

As he went inside, my heart was racing. *Did he just say what I think he said?* Maybe he thinks I'm here for someone else. My father said there wasn't going to be a funeral.

When he came back, I verified my grandmother's name to him again. He confirmed that, in fact, her funeral was on Monday at 11am. He said to come early, like 10am. "I'll be here, I'll close the parlor doors so you can have a moment alone," he assured me. I was speechless. There was going to be a funeral and I was not invited!

Enmity was building in my gut. Before it could fester, I thought that just maybe my father had forgotten to tell me. He wouldn't deliberately leave me out when he knew how much Freshy meant to me and how much I meant to her. As the guy was locking the rear door, I thanked him and walked back around to the front of the building, hopped in my car, and drove back to school.

On the weekends I normally went home to be with Devin, but my spirit was vexed, my heart was broken, I was depressed. I wanted to be alone. Since I had my dorm room to myself, I went back there and cried myself to sleep. I had a ton of sticky notes on my door, missed calls from my mother and father. I didn't want my mother to worry, so I used my neighbor's room phone and called my mother to assure her that I was alright. I told her I went to the viewing and I was gravely devastated and needed time alone. She tried cheering me before hanging up the phone. Still no mention of a funeral.

Saturday and Sunday, I contemplated what I was going to do about going to the funeral. I decided I was definitely going. I laid out my outfit, my friend let me borrow her long black dress and black leather knee boots. My knee-length deep-red wool-coat with the drastic full-wide-hood that overlapped with a tie belt, it was the perfect head-turning ensemble. I purchased a pair of blacked-out oversized Jackie-O shades and found my satin, maroon and black scarf. My goal was to turn heads and have everyone whispering, "Who's that?" The secret was coming out, and there was no turning back.

Monday morning on my way there, it was cold, dark, and cloudy outside. It had rained on and off since the night before and nothing makes a winter morning more depressing than dark clouds and cold rain. I got stuck in traffic and got lost. By the time I arrived, people were already there, walking up the steps to go inside. I missed my opportunity again, to see Freshy privately.

I parked directly across the street from the funeral home, and just as I was putting my satin scarf on my head to tie it around my neck—just as Marilyn

Monroe wore hers—I saw two black limos pull up, parallel to my car. The street was wide and double-laned, so there was a great distance between them and me. Several ushers came from inside the funeral home and walked to the first car with umbrellas. When one usher got to the first limo, I knew it was my father, his wife, and their daughter. I was a nervous wreck. I couldn't make out the people coming out of the second limo; several of them had canes.

All weekend, I had hoped the maintenance man was wrong and I had received misinformation. But this was, in fact, a funeral; a well-planned funeral. I looked in my rearview mirror, put my sunglasses and ruby red lipstick on, and told God it was about to get ugly.

When I walked into the funeral home, the foyer was empty. My father and his family had already gone inside. I thought maybe I should make a grand entrance and bust open the double doors that led into the parlor. I could swirl my coat around and make my presence known. I couldn't decide if I should be dramatic and angry or dramatic and sad. Sure, I would look as if I was intoxicated, but I was hurt. Betrayal came to mind. I had been lied to, again, and counted out.

The moment I grabbed both knobs, the usher from the inside grabbed the doors and opened the left side for me. I was immediately overtaken by the large crowd. It humbled me. A crippling pain seized my stomach as if I had eaten something ninety days past its expiration date.

The large parlor was cramped with so many people in attendance. I stood in the back, lost. I saw the back of my father's head, with his wife and daughter sitting next to him in the front row. Every bit of confidence from only moments before escaped me. I started breathing heavily, and could barely catch my breath. As my self-esteem deflated like a balloon, it was redundantly evident that I was a lifelong secret —the illegitimate child.

I noticed a few of my grandmother's friends and people who worked with my father. I saw a guy who resembled my father, and knew he had to be my brother.

The usher leaned in and asked if I was ready to be seated. I shook my head yes. She directed me to sit in the back of the funeral home, on the far right. My blood was boiling, getting hotter by the minute. An array of emotions was hitting me at once. Anger toward my father. Fear of doing something that could put me in jail. Contempt for not being included.

Then, it hit me, Freshy was gone. Melancholy music played softly as people walked up to the casket to view her body and pay final respects.

Before the funeral director approached the podium to start the service, my father's best friend got up from his seat three rows in front of me and came to sit next to me. He put his arms around me and told me everything was going to be okay. I whispered back I was fine. My father turned around and noticed it was me. Behind the shades and the scarf, he knew it was me. He got up from his seat and headed toward us, walking up the center aisle. As he approached, his friend got up to let my father sit next to me. He asked me if I was okay. I didn't respond. I was numb. I was mad. Tears were bursting out my eyes and running down my face like a waterfall.

My father removed my glasses and pulled my scarf back so that it looked like a neck scarf and not a dramatic disguise. He took his handkerchief from the inside of his suit jacket and wiped my eyes, but the cold tears kept coming. It was as if I was sitting next to a stranger. I was uncertain of everything at that moment. My thoughts were clouded. *Is this how I'm going to spend the rest of my life…in secrecy? Will I relive this scene when he dies?*

As the music stopped, my father stood up, grabbed

my hand, and we walked together down the middle aisle toward the front row. A giant wave of redemption and relief came over me. This was the moment I had longed for my entire life. It took my grandmother's death for him to acknowledge my existence to his wife. I was leaping for joy on the inside. Then, he stopped. Two rows behind where his other family was sitting, he directed me to sit on the end of the aisle, two rows behind him and them. He then walked back to his seat as the soloist started singing.

The longer I sat in that seat with his family two rows in front of me, it felt like we were the only ones sitting in the entire parlor. It seemed as if I was in a bad dream. My foot was shaking and I wanted to scream at the top of my lungs.

I glanced over and saw all of my grandmother's friends from the block, sitting in the front row on the right side of the chapel. They were the ones who had gotten out of the limo. My father sent a limo to Philadelphia to pick her *friends* up, but I didn't get invited. Several of them looked over at me and waved eagerly. Some were blowing kisses. I was wishing my father hadn't taken my glasses off.

I couldn't sit still, so when the Pastor asked if anyone had any final words, I stood up. I slowly walked down the remaining aisle, contemplating what I should say or do. I went up to Freshy's casket and whispered, "I love you," near her right ear. I took my scarf from around my neck and laid it on her chest. I kissed her cold dead body and walked past the front row where my father was sitting with his family. I held my head up high, pushed open the double doors, and busted out the funeral home, leaving a loud sound behind me as the doors slammed. I ran to my car and got myself together by speaking affirmations that I was better than the third row. I was worth more than the way I had been treated. I was not defined by the secrecy in which I was kept.

It took me some time to calm down. I drove to my mother's job not far from the funeral home, and dropped off Freshy's obituary with the receptionist. I didn't want to have a conversation about what happened so I left a note with the obituary, that I'd call her later. I went back to my dorm, took a nap and woke up to several messages that my father had called the dorm payphone in the hallway. I was determined that he was going to have to sweat this one out. I wasn't going to speak to him until I was ready. Bank deposits or gold jewelry, were his go to gifts when he knew he messed up. There wasn't enough money in the world to make me pick up the phone. I wanted more.

CHAPTER FOUR

When I found out I was pregnant in high school, I wasn't ready to be a mom. In fact, I went to get an abortion. I gathered every dime I could and woke up at the crack of dawn to get to an abortion clinic forty minutes from home. I remember spending hours in the waiting room, seeing the counselor, getting an ultrasound, and then waiting to be put to sleep with local anesthesia. I just wanted to feel like myself again.

After the ultrasound, it was determined that I was further along than I thought, and the process was going to cost more than what I had on me. When they told me to come back the following week, I was devastated. I cried the whole way home. I didn't have any more money, and the baby's father had already given me a shoebox full of his savings. I thought long and hard about how I was going to come up with the extra money, or hide the pregnancy to later give the baby up for adoption. There was no way I could be a teen mom.

I went home and as soon as my grandmother met me at the door, she clearly had something to get off her chest and wasted no time. "I know you're pregnant! I prayed when you left here that whatever you went to do with that money you held in your hand while you slept, that plan would fail." I was silent as she continued to tell me that I had until dinnertime to tell my mom I was pregnant.

Later that evening, after dinner, I got the nerve to tell my mom. She pleaded that abortion was a sin and said that she would help care for the baby. She said that God would make a way. She assured me that my life wasn't over.

In return, I pleaded that I wasn't ready to be a mom. When I suggested giving up the baby for adoption, she offered to raise the baby until I finished college and got on my feet.

* * * * *

After Freshy's funeral is when I really rebelled and lost my way. I dropped out of college, started hanging in the streets, making money illegally, and found a Clyde who needed a Bonnie. Deep inside I was hurting, but everything I was being introduced to was the perfect distraction from the chaos I was feeling on the inside. I didn't wake up one day and decide to rebel against my parents. It happened gradually.

My mother and stepfather were going through a separation. They had agreed to keep Devin while I went to college, but after my stepfather moved out, my mom could no longer care for Devin. My father and I weren't on speaking terms. I had no choice but to find my own way.

My older sister called shortly after Freshy died. She said I needed to come get Devin from my mother's house; I needed to take care of my responsibilities. She argued that my mother shouldn't have to care for my child while I was off at college. I rebutted, "But, that was the agreement…" She voiced that I was selfish and called me a bunch of names that portrayed me as a deadbeat mother.

After picking Devin up from my mom's, I returned to school that night with my boy and all of his belongings. I had no idea at that point who was going to keep him while I went to class, or while I worked, but just about everyone on my floor helped. They watched Devin while I went to class, and kept his existence hidden from the RA.

A guy my cousin had introduced me to during my first semester called me up one day. We grew to be really close friends. He often snuck into my dormitory through the laundry room window, to watch Devin for me. My college was an all-girl school and if he was caught in my room without signing in, I'd be in a lot of trouble. By the end of that semester, we were girlfriend and boyfriend and he took care of Devin as if he was his own child. His mom, sister and brother considered Devin as part of their family. That summer after school was out, I moved into his mom's house with him in South Philly.

While working at the mall, I ran into a girl from church. She told me she was making good money 'dancing'. She said I'd make enough to get whatever I needed and wanted for Devin and myself. I was intrigued. All I wanted was my own place, and enough money to send Devin to daycare while I went back to college in the fall. She told me I could do that plus more. It was the perfect solution.

The first night as a dancer I felt like a piece of meat in a lion's den. The touching, grabbing, pulling, and lustful looks were overwhelming. I had no idea what I was doing or how to respond to all the attention. The girl from church had made it sound so easy: change into sexy underwear and a sexy bra; prance around the lounge; when a guy wants to dance, he'll ask you. One lap dance for the duration of one song in exchange for $10—that was easy! Being gawked over, disrespected, and called without use of my name wasn't easy to adjust to, not to mention I had to drown out my subconscious thoughts telling me what I was doing was wrong.

That night I was asked over a half dozen times if I was interested in 'dating'. Each time, I responded, "I have a boyfriend."

When I linked up with the girl from church in the bathroom and told her I had made $100 in an hour, she congratulated me and told me that was good for a first timer. I expressed that I was flattered to be asked if I wanted to go on a date so many times. She said that's another way to make a quick hundred dollars. Confused again, I questioned how so, and she explained that dating was short for 'a quickie in the car or back alley'. I had no idea. It was evidence of my naivete.

I left the lounge that night with a little over $300,

without 'dating'. I started making about $600 a week with just two nights of dancing. In addition to my day job, I had more than enough money to get my own place, pay for daycare, and go back to school. Instead of struggling to make ends meet, I was trying to figure out how I could flip the money I was earning to do bigger things, like purchase my first home and buy a laundromat I had my eye on. My boyfriend was the perfect person to help me do it, because he had connections. The only thing was, I had to reveal my nighttime job to him.

Dancing nights was innocent enough at first, but soon I managed to turn it into dancing and dealing. I'd hint to every guy I gave a lap dance that I also had something extra. The system we set up was working well. We'd travel from clubs in Philly to New Jersey and the money was pouring in, until girls started getting brutally raped by beer bottles and clubs had to tighten security; some clubs even shut down. It pushed us to hustle in the streets. The more I danced and the more he hustled on the streets, the more we bought to re-up. That's when the trouble started— from being chased by a car with a firing Uzi to running in and out of crack houses for supply, traveling state to state with 'weight', carrying a gun to work for protection, constantly watching over my shoulder, and an attempted kidnapping after my boyfriend was a main suspect for murder. Fear was settling in deep and I was realizing I wanted more from life, but I was dangerously in love in with my first love.

Eventually, my father and I started speaking again. It started the day he recalled dragging me out of South Philly. When he told the story, you'd think he had busted into my boyfriend's house and pulled me out by my hair, kicking and screaming. Great storyteller! What actually happened, was my father showed up at my boyfriend's house in Philly where I had been hiding out. Now, to his credit, he did bang on the door to the point the vibration made the walls shake, and he did yell while threatening me to come outside. If you're wondering how he knew where I was, to this day that remains a mystery.

I was shaken when I heard the banging on the door. I looked out the front bedroom window and the first thing I spotted was my father's car. I'm just like my father—we don't give up—defeat is not an option. I knew he wasn't going to leave until I came downstairs. The banging continued until I yelled, "One moment!"

When I opened the door in a pair of short shorts and a tank top, he said, "Put some damn clothes on and get in the car. I'm taking you home."

"You just can't come here and make me go home! I'm not *that* daughter!"

"Young lady, don't make me hurt you. Your son hasn't seen you in days, and your mother is beside herself with worry. Get in the damn car."

I stood there with an attitude.

He repeated, in a louder tone, "Girl, I'm not playing with you. GET THE HELL IN THE CAR!!" My father had never yelled at me like that before, and it actually startled me.

"What about my car?" I whined.

"Where is it?"

"My boyfriend took his mother to the store; they'll be back."

He was livid. His anger went from level five to fifty-five. He walked out the house, yelling, "He better get here fast, or I'll report the car stolen."

As my father walked to his car, I started talking to myself out loud while gathering my belongings. "This boy better hurry up and I hope to God he parks a block away."

Ten minutes went by, and he hadn't arrived yet. My father walked back inside the house and said, "I'll tow your car home. Let's go, I'm not waiting no more." He meant business.

By the time I grabbed my belongings, my boyfriend had parked a few cars behind my father's car. His mom wasn't with him. There was no time for questions. I immediately ran to him, told him to give me the keys and that I had to go. I also told him to walk around the corner; I didn't want my father to see him.

I hopped in my car, pulled alongside my father's, honked the horn signaling I was ready, and made my way over to my mom's house in New Jersey. When we arrived, my father told me to go upstairs and get washed up, like I was a child. I didn't even argue. I walked upstairs, took a shower, and under the hot water, I cried. It was as if he had rescued me. Suddenly, being a secret didn't matter. His wife and son not knowing about my existence seemed minor. I had seen and done so much; I was just blessed and thankful to be home. I will forever be grateful to God for his grace and mercy.

When I came downstairs, we all sat in the living room and my father told me that Freshy had left me some money. I was surprised. He wanted me to use it to get on my feet, so he said he would get me an apartment and put it in his name. He'd take care of everything until I got a job and got settled. He kept his promise. Aside from helping with the rent, he visited every other weekend to buy groceries and take Devin on car rides. Devin was young and I felt the need to prepare him as my mother had prepared me. I told him if he saw Pop-Pop while we were out, he couldn't speak to him. I told him Pop-Pop had another family that didn't know about us. He was too young to understand, but I knew, like me, one day he'd get it.

Several years later, I got a really good job, working in a hotel office. My relationship with my father went from him fathering me and taking care of me to becoming my friend. Over the years, we spent a lot of time together, especially while I was working at the luxury hotel he loved in downtown Philadelphia. He was so proud that I had a job, and an office job at that. My first week there, he took me to Lord and Taylor to get a few suits, then to PNC to open a bank account.

The hotel I was working for was urban fancy. They played jazz music in the lobby, and on the phone when you were on hold—blues jazz the kind that you would pay top dollar to get a back row seat just to listen to. My father loved jazz, the good stuff. Miles Davis on trombone, Jimmy Cobb on tenor sax, Ella Fitzgerald scatting away. I remember jazz records playing in our apartment often when I was young. There were several times he'd pick me up to go to lunch, and he'd say, "You gotta get me your hotel's hold music on CD." On Father's Day that year, I gave him the Pottery Barn's CD, "Dinner at Eight". He was thrilled, and I mean really thrilled. He was blushing when he opened the gift. I don't think I ever saw him so excited. Wait. I take that back. I saw him very excited four years later, the day that my now-husband asked him for my hand in marriage.

I told my father I had met a really nice guy, and I wanted them to meet. I asked if he would meet us at my mom's house. He agreed. I had never asked my father to meet any of my boyfriends before. He had taken the opportunity to curse-out my former boyfriend from Philly, run him out of my apartment, and tell him not to ever come near me again. I hopped in and out of bad relationships looking for love, until a girl at my job re-introduced me to the love of my life, God. The healing began. I experienced verbal abuse, physical abuse, sexual abuse but Ronney was different; he was the one. Not only did he know the Lord, but he also prayed for me, he catered to me, and I hung onto every word he spoke into me. He protected me. He saw me. He won my heart because he wanted the best for my soul. That beautiful day in November, my father met the man I knew I was going to marry. He suggested we take a ride. I hopped in the back seat and Ronney sat in front. We drove up to Fort Dix military base.

The last time I had been to Fort Dix was when my father had broken my heart. There were no good vibes as we pulled into the parking space outside the PX. The walk through the parking lot was draining my energy as I remembered that awkward moment when my father had denied who I was. In the present, he and Ronney were talking about aircraft, since Ronney was a pilot and my father was a retired Air Force Vet.

Determined not to relive the past, I grabbed a shopping cart. Ronney leaned over to me and asked if he could get some time alone with my father. I said sure, and went shopping on the other side of the commissary for a few things. Not long after I left them alone, I bumped into them several aisles over and found my father with a huge smile on his face. He looked at me and said, "This is the one, huh?"
I laughed and replied, "I think so, Daddy. I absolutely think so." He laughed and smiled. Ronney had asked my father for my hand in marriage, or as he calls it, he notified him of the 'change in command'. The same place where years ago my father denied who I was to him, ironically was the same place where my husband confirmed to my father that he would love, honor, protect, and cherish me forever.

Planning the wedding was easy—my parents came together and both contributed. Even though putting an announcement in the newspaper wasn't an option for me, I was content. To my benefit, engagement websites were the new trend anyway. On our personal site it was safe to announce our wedding and mention my father by his full name. The only way his wife would find out was if she googled him, to my knowledge she wasn't too savvy on the computer.

Throughout the entire planning process, I was fearful that my father would not show up to the wedding. Growing up, there were many times he would make promises to be there, and many times he was not. His heart and intentions were in the right place, but somehow things would pop up and he'd call and say he couldn't make it. Eventually, I grew accustomed to hoping for the best while expecting very little.

When I asked God for a wedding date, October 1st dropped into my spirit. It just happened to fall on a Sunday. Sundays were my father's only day off from work. I was relieved that I didn't have to compete with his work; my real competition was his family, and whether he could get out of the house for an entire day. I asked him at least once a month for eleven months if he was going to be at the wedding. Every time, he replied, "Babe, I'm going to be there."
"The whole day, Daddy? The whole day?"
"The whole day, babe, the whole day!"

A month or so before the wedding, Ronney and his groomsmen went to get fitted for their tuxedos. Ron called me to say my father had called him and canceled. I was an emotional wreck, and I couldn't call him until Monday when I knew he was at work. He had never given me his house number and he didn't have a cell phone.

Monday couldn't come soon enough. When I got to work, my father had left me a voicemail, telling me he was going to come to my job and pick me up for lunch at noon, to meet him near the hotel's valet. *LUNCH?!* I thought. *You need your tuxedo, sir!*

The hours that morning crawled by. I called my mom and told her that there was a strong chance my father was on his way to my job to let me know over lunch that he wasn't coming to the wedding. She said with confidence, "Heather, he will be there. Don't you worry!" My mother always had an optimistic view of everything; she believed the best in people because she gave her best to people. I didn't believe her, and I spent the morning preparing myself for the letdown he was going to deliver when he arrived at noon. I told myself repetitively, "It's okay if he doesn't make it, and it's okay if he doesn't walk you down the aisle." I prayed and asked God to grant me serenity and grace to accept whatever the outcome.

Finally, it was almost noon. I waited by the valet for only a minute and as always, he was on time. When I hopped in the car, he said, "I'm going to go to the tuxedo place down the street. I need you to sit in the car while I run inside to get fitted."

I tried to play it cool—"Oh, okay!"—but the moment he got out of the car and went into the shop, I shouted, "THANK YOU, JESUUUUUUS!!"

Getting a parking space in downtown Philadelphia on a weekday is almost impossible, so double parking on the street with someone seated on the passenger side was the best bet. When he hopped back in the car, he said, "I'm letting you know now, I'm only wearing those cheap shoes for one hour! After that, I'm changing into my own shoes."

I told him he could wear slippers, just as long as he was there. He promised, "I wouldn't miss it for the world, babe." He slapped my knee and said, "Don't worry, I'll be there."

We laughed about those plastic shoes all the way to his favorite, Famous Deli on 4th street in South Philly for lunch. There was no better way to celebrate, "the father of the bride," like a Philly sub.

On October 1, 2006, my father walked me down the aisle and gave me away at the altar. After the wedding, the entire wedding party walked a few blocks to City Hall from the hotel, and the photographer took pictures of us walking up the street. My father had on his brown Wallabies with his tuxedo. The combination looked nice. I could tell once we were done taking pictures and got back to the hotel, he was in a rush—he wanted to know the schedule of events for the reception.

I told the wedding planner my father was anxious to get home. She arranged the daddy-daughter dance to be immediately after the bride and groom's first dance. As he and I two-stepped to Beyoncé's "Daddy" in the center of the floor, my hand in his, I took in every movement. At that moment, it was a dream come true. Then, he asked how much longer the song was. I said, "Dad, it's three minutes, you've got three more minutes!"

"Yeah, my feet hurt, that's all."

As the song wrapped up, I started to sing along:

"I know it ain't easy
Men who take care of their responsibilities
Love is overwhelming
All that you did pay for me,
Can't stop my tears from falling
I love you so much, Daddy
Thank you (I want my unborn son to be like my
Daddy)
You've done so much for me (I want my husband to
be like my Daddy)
I love you, Daddy."

My father had great qualities. If I wasn't his secret, I'd probably have thought he was the perfect parent. His wisdom, calm demeanor and tone, and the ability to take control of things so I wouldn't have to even think about them, were qualities I loved. I wanted my husband and son to harbor those traits, in addition to being the men that they were called to be by God. It was the perfect song for a perfect day.

After we danced, he had to go. He told me everything was beautiful and to call him when I returned from the honeymoon.

CHAPTER FIVE

Several months later, Ronney and I were shopping for items to decorate our baby nursery. I had complications early in the pregnancy; it's how we found out so soon that we were expecting. We were standing near the glass showcase when my cell phone rang. It was my father's best friend. He said, "Heather, I got bad news to tell you."

"What?! What is it?"

"Your father suffered a heart attack and a stroke."

I was crippled with fear and devastation, and worst of all, I couldn't run to be by his side. I dropped the phone, and Ronney picked it up and said, "Hello?" My father's friend introduced himself as the guy that came to the wedding with my father. He continued, "Ronney, things don't look good. I'll keep you posted, please pray and take care of Heather."

It became difficult for me to breathe as I heard him

utter those words through the speaker. I ran out of the store, then started pacing back and forth. I tried praying, but I was too overwhelmed. Ronney let me pace a few times before he stopped me and said, "Breathe!" Right there on the sidewalk in front of the hobby store, Ronney began to pray for my father and me. He declared that my father was going to be alright. He assured me that God was not done with him. He said, "There's too much that's unfinished. God is going to allow him to live. Every prayer you ever prayed concerning your father is in the will of God, and shall come to pass."

I received every word my husband spoke. This wasn't how God promised me the story would end. Immediately, I had peace knowing my father couldn't die, and I was still his secret. I also remembered that when one of my cousins died unexpectedly, God had promised that I'd never be blindsided by death again.

Trusting God's word without visible evidence takes faith. I exercised my faith starting that night. I convinced my mind that things were different than what I heard. I believed that, "He shall live and not die." Two weeks later, I got a call from my father's friend letting me know that my father was out of the ICU and recovering. I wanted to see him, but obviously I couldn't. I needed to talk to him, but obviously I couldn't. Instead, I told his best friend to let him know I was praying for him every night and that I was confident that he would be completely healed. I continued, "This is a light affliction and better days are coming."

He said, "I'm going to tell him, and don't worry, he's a fighter. He loves you, Heather. Don't stress, and take care of that baby." I promised him that I was not worried. I already knew the outcome.

Three months went by with no word from my father. I kept my faith and remained optimistic. When he finally called, I was ecstatic to hear from him, but he was talking very fast and barely allowed me to get a word in. He said his wife had run to the store and he didn't have much time to talk. He expressed that he was going to get a cell phone so that he could call me on Tuesdays and Thursdays when he went to physical therapy. Before he hung up, he said that he felt my prayers and loved me very much. "I'll talk to you soon, babe," and before I could respond, he hung up.

I was so excited to hear his voice, to know that he was okay, I didn't care that the call lasted under sixty seconds, or that our new terms of communication were two days a week while he was at physical therapy. The relief of knowing he was on the road to recovery was comfort enough. God had heard my prayers.

That summer, Ronney and I welcomed our baby boy, Malachi. My father was unable to come see him when he was born, so he had his friend deposit money into my bank account. When I had my first son, Devin, my father came to the hospital with enough diapers and formula to last an entire year, no exaggeration. He was disappointed that I was a teen mom at the time, but after the shock wore off, he and my mother came up with a plan to make sure Devin was taken care of. Back then, he'd take Devin for a ride on Sundays. Sunday rides with Pop-Pop, Devin used to call it. I wanted Malachi to have that same experience, but unfortunately, my father was no longer driving himself around, and he was forced to retire due to his inability to do his job. At best, all my baby would have were weekly phone calls when his Pop-Pop would go to physical therapy.

Just as we were getting acclimated to the new schedule, I was on break at work and noticed seven missed calls on my cell phone—five from a New Jersey phone number, and two from my father. It was strange for him to call so early in the day and not on a Tuesday or Thursday, so I automatically assumed something bad had happened. I walked outside and called the unknown number first, no answer and then the phone rang, it was my father. When I answered there was silence, so I said again, "Hello?!"

My father whispered, "Stay near your phone, I'm going to call you back later. Don't answer any calls from any unknown phone numbers." I said okay and asked if everything was okay. He whispered, "No, babe, it's not good. Just be sure to not answer if anyone calls you from a number you don't know, and stay by your phone."

"Okay!" I suspiciously replied. We hung up.

Not long after, my phone rang. Again it was a New Jersey number I didn't know. I was uncertain if my father was testing me, so I let it ring.

Finally, my shift was over and Ronney came to pick me up. Normally I walked home from work, but that day he wanted to come and get me. Before I could buckle my seatbelt and put my purse in the backseat, my father called. "Babe, I got some bad news."

"WHAT IS IT?!"

"My wife found out about you, and she's really angry. It's a madhouse in here."

I couldn't believe it. *Finally*, I thought. Of course she's mad. Thirty-two years is a long time to keep a secret that you have another child. He continued, "That was her, calling you. She wants answers, but don't you worry about it, I have to find a way to fix this. The thing is, I don't know the next time I'll be able to talk to you; she's going to be on me like a hawk."

Just before hanging up, he apologized. "Babe, I never meant to hurt you, my wife, or your mother. This is my problem to solve. I'll talk to you as soon as I can. I love you."

"I love you, Daddy."

It was a lot to process. I had always imagined that when his wife found out about me, it would feel GOOD. I thought I would feel a huge weight lifted off of me. As it turned out, I put my feet in her "expensive shoes" as a married woman. I had never considered the whole situation as a wife—how devastating it would be to find out that your spouse had fathered an 'outside' child, then lied about it for over three decades. I never thought about how she would feel, being that they never had a child together. I actually felt sad for her now.

As a child, I hadn't thought of her feelings or any of that. When I was a young girl, I only ever wanted my father to tell his wife about me. It's funny, the bible says, *"When I was a child I thought as a child but when I grew old, I put away my childish things."* That day that my father's wife found out about me was the first time I ever prayed for her— as a woman, as a wife. I prayed that God would heal her. I prayed that God would keep her heart in his hands and restore her strength while renewing her mind and soul. I prayed that He would mend what was broken and do it expeditiously. I prayed that He would dull the pain, give her comfort, and that she would find serenity in knowing that this too shall pass. Lastly, I prayed that their marriage would weather this storm and forgiveness would be their testimony as to how they made it through.

Six months or so passed by before I heard from my father again. He said that things had been really rough at home. He didn't mention how he had rectified the situation or how his wife had handled such devastating news. He carried on as if all was well.

At that time, I was working about fifteen minutes from where they lived. He said he'd try to schedule to meet up with me at least once a week at the mall. He was driving again, so weekly lunch at the mall replaced our previous Tuesday and Thursday phone calls.

Soon after, Ronney's job relocated us to Arizona. When I told my father that we were moving, he was excited for us. He had a war buddy who lived out there and he said maybe he'd come and visit all of us. His optimism was comforting, but I knew that with the oxygen machine he carried around and troubles at home, he was only trying to make me feel at ease with moving across the country away from all my family and friends. He promised to find a way to call me as often as possible.

CHAPTER SIX

Three months after we arrived in Arizona, Ronney was deployed overseas as a contractor for nine months. It was just me and our boys in a new town 2,551 miles away from family and friends. We all matured and grew within. I started to get in shape. Every week, I could be found going mountain climbing, cycling, running, lifting weights at the gym, meeting new friends who became family, traveling, and healing emotional wounds that were attached to my insecurities. I never felt so good about who I was and the woman I was becoming.

A few years later, Ronney was laid off. We started out with a pretty hefty savings account, so we weren't concerned at first, but as time passed the financial frustrations, and all those months apart began to take a toll on us and our marriage. Things were tough, and by the time we hit rock bottom we had exhausted our savings to the point we were homeless. We signed up for welfare, moved into a motel with the boys, and worked low paying jobs just to get by. It didn't get us far. We stretched the money we made as far as we could.

I knew my father would help, since my birthday was only weeks away. I called him out of desperation. "Dad?"

He sounded concerned. "Hey, is everything alright?"

"We've hit a rough patch here. Is there any way you can gift me a few hundred dollars for my birthday? I really need it." He asked me for my bank account number, and soon after he finished repeating it, he said, "Alright I got it. I'll send it by the end of the day. Is everything okay?"

I told him everything was fine and not to worry. We hung up.

Later that afternoon, he sent more than I had asked for, and it was more than enough to get the kids some things they wanted.

The next day, while I was at work, I had several missed calls from my father and a voice message. On the message he said, "If my wife calls, tell her that you don't know me." As I listened, he was calling the other line. I clicked over, and he asked me if I got his message. I lied and said I hadn't heard it yet. "What's going on, Dad?" My heart was racing.

He said his wife found out about the money he deposited into my account, and he repeated what he said on the voicemail in the same panicked tone: "If she calls you, tell her you don't know me!"

Did I really just hear my father say what I think he said?! I couldn't believe it. My father was asking me to lie. My father was asking me to compromise my feelings for his wife's feelings. *I thought she knew about me. Why would I tell her otherwise?*

With barely enough energy to speak, I said, "Sure." At that moment, I realized my mom was right nineteen years prior, when she called my father a coward. I hung up the phone. I didn't say goodbye or express my disappointment. Tears fell uncontrollably from my eyes, pity was pushed out by anger, and over thirty years of pent-up emotions came pouring out. Rage had set in. I WAS PISSED! I called him back and there was no answer.

I walked away from my desk at work and took a walk outside. I belted out a shout from my gut and continued walking, pacing the parking lot back and forth. The sun was beaming on my back. My vision started to blur. My heart was racing as the phone rang. It was him. I hit decline. It rang again, I hit decline. I knew if I accepted that call, I'd say things my pride would never let me apologize for. If I never spoke to him again, I would be fine. Every time he called me, I declined his calls. I called my mom and took my frustration out on her. Everything I wanted to say to him, I said to her. I was too old to be dealing with their mess, too old to be denied, too old to be crying over the words my father said to me, but they stung, they penetrated my soul. "Tell her you don't know me." One phrase did enough damage that I felt hate toward my father for the first time. I was emotionally exhausted.

CHAPTER SEVEN

Spiritually broken, financially broke, marriage in shambles, and thousands of miles away from home, my life felt screwed. My girlfriends were determined to keep my spirit up, every Sunday they held a prayer conference call. Each of us took turns praying over one another. Carla prays strategically, she reminds me of Deborah in the bible her gift is Spiritual Warfare, and Samantha travails, she's more of a Hannah in the bible, she prays with supplication. Their prayers were essential in this season of my life.

Ronney decided to switch churches for more in-depth teaching about God. He found a small church in our town that taught a huge message every Sunday. I could feel my strength being restored as I learned how to navigate through the bible and activate my faith once again.

At this point, Ronney and I were in toleration mode. He was feeling like a failure because he was unable to provide for us. We took our frustrations out on each other, we saw hard times before, but this was by far the worse. I simply wanted out; I was tired of being tired. The weight I had lost came back, I didn't look or feel like myself, my credit score was plummeting and even though the boys never mentioned their disappointment, I felt like we had failed them.

One Sunday, the assistant pastor of the church introduced herself to us, and Ronney asked her if the church had marriage counseling. As it turned out, she was a marriage counselor. I wasn't interested, so I walked off. When Ronney got in the car, he told me he'd made an appointment for us to speak with her in a few days. I was furious. We had just gotten to the church, and now we were going to dump our lives in their hands? It took me several days to calm down and wrap my mind around the idea of getting advice from someone we knew nothing about. I had done the counseling thing all throughout school: counselors and therapists, therapists and counselors. I didn't have much faith in it working. Nothing was going to change. I decided to prove to him that it was a waste of time, so I went.

After a few months of therapy, Ronney had a job offer back east that included a relocation package. Great—just as we were making positive progress. I was actually enjoying counseling. Every week we had exercises and tasks to work on. Working on us felt good. We were laughing again, getting closer, the intimacy was refreshing. I had my best friend back. I decided to stay in Arizona and let the kids finish school. I also took the counselor's offer to continue seeing her one on one. I was carrying so much emotional weight; I admitted that I needed help. We started from my first recollection of trauma. I knew what she was going to dig up: being molested. She wanted to take me on a journey of recalling my most memorable experiences. I could play it out in my head like it happened yesterday but saying it out loud was something different.

I was playing with toys, a dollhouse to be exact, at a family member's house. My cousin and I were six or seven years old at the time. We had to dig up the pieces from the basement because the set had belonged to their older sibling. As we searched for all the pieces of the doll house, we found some faux food to play with as well. In excitement, we kept running upstairs to the living room to lay everything out. As I was holding the peas, I heard my name called from upstairs. I was fearful, so I pretended I didn't hear him calling me, and I kept playing. Then

he called again, in a stern voice, "Heather, come here!"
I got up and headed toward the steps.

It was a sunny afternoon; the natural light was the only light in the house. The closer I got upstairs, the darker it got. My cousin was still playing with the faux food pretending to feed the dolls. As I got to the top step he pulled me into a bedroom, pushed me in the closet and told me to open my mouth. The smell of body funk, feet, and urine made me want to vomit. As I told the counselor step by step what happened in that closet, I realized at that moment that it wasn't the first time I was made to do this. It had happened before.

The counselor told me to close my eyes and go back to the room. "Look around and tell me what you see." I said I saw the sun piercing through the window, the glare almost blinding out the furniture in the room. As I stared at the gazing sun, I started to cry. I knew what that meant. God was present. As I relived that moment when I ran down the steps and the sun was glaring through the front window, God was there. I wept and wept and wept some more in my counselor's house, on her floral velour sofa. Tears flowed from deep in my soul until all I could do was moan from my diaphragm. With every groan, the pain of that young Heather, lifted. The pain of young

Heather who didn't understand the sexual urges she prematurely felt after being molested, departed. The pain of young adult Heather who loosely gave herself away because she didn't understand her worth, departed. God was there. God was there!

I know you may be thinking, "If God was there why would He allow it." The bible says God never leaves us or forsakes us. It wasn't for me to understand 'why'. *Why me?!* I had just recently come to the understanding that before I was in my mother's womb, my spirit had a task that needed to be fulfilled on this earth. According to statistics 1 in 6 women in the U.S. are sexually assaulted. It wasn't about what happened to me, as much as it was about getting over what happened to me. Decades of my life I spent scared of tight-dark places, questioning my judgement, and self-worth, blaming myself, trying to understand why I was sexually awkward, and as an adult why was I holding on to the secret to protect my family. I needed to forgive, in spite of the fact that the same person who violated me as a child approached me later as an adult with inappropriate requests and gestures. That's what I hated the most, the nerve of adding salt to the injury. Nonetheless, I had to forgive in order to make peace with it, heal from it, and eventually, help others. Understanding that God was present in the midst of trouble was comforting more than confusing.

Every week in my counselor's home, we peeled back layers of hurt and pain. We uncovered the dysfunction I normalized. Right around the time that I found peace and accepted healing is when my father called, dumping those devastating words on me: "If my wife calls you, tell her you don't know me." Every strategy my counselor had given me for dealing with unexpected situations, creating boundaries, were all irrelevant in that moment. I needed an emergency session. She agreed to see me.

It was time to deal with the biggest obstacle in my life, my relationship with my father. I often wondered if the chaos I experienced in my life was because I was literally born into sin. Through counseling, I learned that it didn't matter how I was created, or what my parents did. God knew me before I was born, He created plans of hope, peace and prosperity for me! I discovered my worth and how to love myself. Once I realized God's love for me, I cared less how anyone else felt about me. I set boundaries, and finally, I felt whole.

Forgiveness was one of the toughest hurdles I had to jump, but I jumped those suckers like it was natural to me. Forgiving my parents, humbled me in a way I didn't think was possible. I made a series of bad decisions throughout my life based on being broken, and I also had to forgive myself. I realized I wasn't perfect. I had hurt people I loved for my own selfish reasons. The bible clearly states if you forgive other people when they sin against you, your heavenly Father will also forgive you.

I came to peace with the fact that my parents were two good-willed people who had made a series of mistakes. They were not bad people; they had simply made some bad decisions. Just like I made bad decisions in my life that were driven by pain, they had reasons for their choices, and it was not my place to judge them. My position was to love and respect them (Exodus 20:12).

As I was in the process of getting myself together, my father would sometimes call. He left a message each time, "love you babe, call me." I wasn't ready to talk yet. I needed to wait for Holy Spirit to let me know it was time, because I didn't want things to go back to the way they were before. I needed my father to experience the new me and respect the new me.

When I finally answered my father's call, there was dead air for what felt like an hour, but it was only about ten seconds. I started out saying, "Dad, you hurt me and there is no apology to fix that."
He said he never meant to hurt me, and he admitted that the first time his wife found out years ago, he

didn't totally tell the truth, he told her he had just found out he had a child and had been unaware of my existence. That's all she knew until she found out about the deposit he made when I asked him for money. She was suspicious as to why he was giving me money when he claimed, "he didn't know me."

He pleaded that he was working on making things right, his health was failing, and he was going to make sure I was no longer kept in the dark.

"Dad, this has gone on way too long and it isn't healthy for either of us. If you want a relationship with me, I will no longer harbor your secrets."

He agreed that I shouldn't have to, and he respected my terms. As I continued to lay out what I expected for the future, I knew the hardest part would be holding onto my own demands and not giving in just because he seemed incapable of giving what I needed. I told him Ronney had accepted a job back east and we would be moving in a few months.

"I can't wait to see you guys," he said.

I reiterated that if the kids saw him in public, they were going to say hello. They would not hide or pretend their Pop-Pop was a stranger. He laughed and said, "That's fine, babe. All is well."

It felt so invigorating to stand my ground, I remember dancing on the cement stairs after I hung up the call. If I could stand up to my father, I could stand up to anyone. Nothing or no one was going to put me in a box that I had to spend months in therapy to get out of. Never again. I was FREE.

John 8:36. "So if the Son sets you free, you will be free indeed."

CHAPTER EIGHT

Five months after moving back to the east coast, I found out that after more than six years of infertility and several miscarriages, I was pregnant again. This time I was carrying identical twin girls. My father called every week; I could even call him if I felt like it. Everything seemed to be going well, until Ronney and I received devastating news early in the pregnancy. We lost twin A in utero, and the doctors gave twin B a very slim chance of surviving. I was immediately put on bedrest, and obligated to travel two hours once a week to monitor baby B. Just like clockwork, my father called to keep me company on the drive. Most times he'd call afterward as well, just to see how the baby and I were doing.

That March, I was a little past midway through my pregnancy when I traveled to my mother's house and met my father there. Devin was in town from Arizona for his birthday. My father and I must have sat talking on the porch for over four hours. He wanted me to know my family history. He also wanted me to know that I had cousins, that wanted to meet me. I learned my family's history that early spring afternoon. It's a memory I'll treasure forever.

A few days before I went into labor, my father called to say he was getting tired of being sick in his body. He listed that he had survived a stroke, a heart attack, and he had beaten cancer a few years back. "My legs aren't strong, I keep falling, and my lungs keep filling with fluid. Babe, I'm 'bout ready to go home." "GO HOME?! Daddy, no, don't say that," I pleaded. After sobbing through the phone, I conceded and asked him if he knew Jesus Christ as his personal savior.

"Yes."

I asked him if he knew if he was going to heaven. He said, "I am going to heaven, babe."

I told him I wasn't ready just yet, and I apologized for being selfish. I wanted him to meet my daughter, his granddaughter, so he promised to keep fighting.

June 14th, I went to my checkup appointment, and by this time Ronney was driving me. Afterward, the doctor suggested I go down to get started with my paperwork to have one of the hospital's OB/GYNs check me out. I was set to deliver July 22nd earlier than anticipated due to Baby A's positioning. When I sat down to fill out paperwork, the nurse said she could take me back. She took my vitals and discovered that my blood pressure was extremely high. The doctor came in and took my blood pressure again. It was too high. "I'm going to have you sent up to Labor and Delivery. You have preeclampsia, and we need to prep you to deliver the baby now."

By the time they took me upstairs, hooked up an IV, and gave me a shot to prepare my body for early delivery, my father had called and left a message that he himself was in the hospital, again. Ronney called him back and notified him that I would be having the baby early, like in a day or so. When I woke up from a nap, Ronney told me my father was very excited that the baby was coming early.

"You told him I was having the baby??" Ronney had no idea that I knew my father was going to stop fighting to live once he knew the baby was on the way. I tried calling him, but received no answer.

June 16th, our daughter, Genesis Isabella was born, and we made final arrangements for her sister Gabriella Isabel. Genesis and Gabriella were trap twins, the odds of carrying trap twins are one in a million. The odds of either of them surviving were one in a million. Favor was on our side and five days later we were able to take Genesis home. It was an emotional week for us. A few weeks later, my father was admitted into a rehabilitation center not far from where he lived. He called and told me to come visit. Ronney drove us almost five hours to see him. When we pulled into the parking lot, we noticed that the rehabilitation center was named Genesis Healthcare. The center was fancy and high tech. At the reception desk they required Ronney and me to sign-in on the digital pad, and we had to disclose how we knew the patient. I proudly put 'daughter'.

"Babe, I think they just want family, friend, or clergy," Ronney joked.

"I earned this privilege," I testified. We laughed.

After getting off the elevator, we passed the cafeteria that looked like a cafe and adjacent five-star restaurant. Crystal chandeliers led way to two-toned painted hallways and opulent carpeting that resembled royal decor. When we walked into his room, Dad was sitting in his chair, watching the horse races. He noticed us right away. He was so excited, by the look in his eyes, I couldn't tell that he was tired. His nurse was in the room and he introduced us as "his daughter, her old man and his new grandbaby." He was still full of laughter, jokes, and great storytelling. He was thrilled to see Gigi. He couldn't believe how much she resembled Freshy and me. He said he was going to do his best to get a gift for her, and he'd have his friend deposit money into my account on his behalf. Before we left, I told my dad that I forgave him. I wanted him to know that for sure, and that I thanked God for him being my father.

He said, "I love you, I'm proud of you and I wish I would have done better."

On the ride home, I felt whole. It wasn't by coincidence that the center was named Genesis. Genesis means the point or place where something begins, arises, or is derived, it's the beginning, the birth, the formation, the emergence. It was there that I wasn't denied, it was there that I was affirmed, it was there.

A few days later, my father's friend called to tell me that my father's wife wouldn't allow my father to get any money out of the bank to give Genesis a gift. I told him we were fine. He said it really broke my father's heart. I told him I'd call to assure him we were okay.

"Your father knows that," his friend said. "He's just upset he wasn't allowed to show his support for your little girl, his grand-girl."

By the end of the week, I was headed back to the Philadelphia metro area to attend my best friend's baby shower. When I arrived at my mom's house and settled in, she told me my father's friend called and told her my father took ill and was headed to hospice. I tried calling my dad, the phone just kept ringing. I tried calling his friend and received his voicemail. Later that evening I went to visit my grandmother. My mom was there getting her hair done, by my cousin when I got the call from my father's best friend. He said my father had passed away at home earlier that day.

James 1:4. "And let endurance have its perfect result, so that you may be perfect and complete, lacking in nothing."

CHAPTER NINE

The morning after hearing about my father's passing, I reached out to his cousin. He had wanted me to meet her some months back. I told her that my father had died. We immediately connected and we talked and talked. She told me she would call my father's wife and get the funeral information. She assured me there would be no mess, and for certain I could count on being at the funeral and sitting up front with the family.

Moments later, she called back and asked if it was okay if she gave my father's wife my phone number. I said sure. So many thoughts were racing through my head. Over three decades, and this was finally coming to closure. I repeatedly rehearsed what I was going to say.

Late that evening, the phone rang. It was her. My

stomach fluttered with butterflies and my heart was racing. "Hello?" The eight-year-old girl inside of me said, "Hello?" as the naïve child within thought her calling me meant acceptance. I was quickly snapped back to reality when she sternly stated that she was calling to tell me about the funeral services. She spoke matter-of-factly, very sophisticated and proper as if she were talking to a jury—sounding almost rehearsed. She gave me the address to the church where the funeral would be held, and explained that if I wanted to walk in with the family, I needed to meet them outside the church. She proceeded to tell me that my father died at home surrounded by 'his girls,' meaning her, their daughter, and their granddaughter. She added that she didn't know why my father kept me hidden for so long. "I'm uncertain how he felt about you, but he was surrounded by his girls when he passed away."

The conversation was getting colder by the minute, as she started throwing shade. I had so much to say—words that would rip her world apart. Verbal abuse would be putting it mildly for the dialogue playing in my head during that conversation. But nothing came out of my mouth—I punked out. All I could summon in response was that I'd see her at the funeral.
"Oh, so you are coming?"
I gritted my teeth and replied, "Absolutely."
"Oh, okay." She then repeated the name of the

church, the address, and the time. Leaving me no time to say goodbye, she said thank you and hung up the phone.

I was so mad at myself, furious even. *How did I allow this woman to talk to me like I was nothing? How could I just stand by and let her?* I took a few deep breaths.

My mother was staying with me, to help me through the mourning process and with the baby. When I got off the phone, she called me into the other room.
"Let's sit down and talk." She was mourning my father's death as well. They had remained friends up until he passed away. That night, she started reminiscing. She told me how they met and fell in love, how she felt horrible about it, how she got caught up and couldn't leave. I sat and listened to my mom pour her heart out for the first time, in detail, from the day they met to the day it ended over a decade later.

My mom is a caring person with a good heart; she loves hard. She's a cheerleader, loves to laugh, and will scope the earth to bless someone in need. She wasn't looking for a married man; my father wasn't looking for a mistress. They found something in one another that was raw, real, and wrong. As a wife, it was tough to hear the particulars to their relationship.

As a daughter, I was intrigued by it all. I was created by two people in love. It was a lot to process. I didn't judge.

I didn't know what to make of it all, because there was a part of me that wanted to use what my mom told me as ammunition to hurt my father's wife. Hurting her for hurting me sounded like reasonable revenge. Instead, I spent the night praying and asking for strength and grace. I asked God to reveal this woman's heart to me so that I could see her the way He saw her.

On the day of the funeral, we stood outside the church. Ronney, Devin, my maternal grandmother, my aunt, and my sister were all there to support me. My father's cousin was also there with her daughters and her niece. She came over and stood with me. I was surrounded by a force of people who cared for me. They knew my father; he meant something to them as well. To this day, I'm grateful for each of them.

As I stood outside the church waiting to go in, I was greeted by several women who introduced themselves as my father's nieces on his wife's side of the family. They gave me hugs and assured me that I was family. They expressed how much I looked like my father and Freshy. They added that they wished they would have known me sooner, and under better circumstances.

Then, a stretch Cadillac pulled up in front of the church. Dressed in all black with a large, brimmed hat, his wife got out, straightened her clothes, and walked toward me. Her daughter and granddaughter followed. She asked if I was Heather.
"Yes, I am."
She told me to follow behind them (her, her daughter, and granddaughter). "Let's put him to rest." Her demeanor was different. She seemed kinder, and her voice was much softer than before.

As we all walked into the church, all the drama at bay, it suddenly hit me that my father was gone. My daddy was gone. I would never hear his voice call me "Babe" again. Our story, our complicated melody over the rhythm of jazz was complete. This was a promise fulfilled by GOD. The day I had feared for so long was right now, my present, and so far it wasn't a nightmare.

Everyone else went around for a final viewing, but I stood in front of my father's casket unable to move, my heart racing a mile a minute. I simply whispered, "I love you, and you were right, it all worked out." As the tears fell down my face and under my chin, I felt someone put their arm around me but couldn't tell who it was. Then I felt another arm reach around me. It was my father's daughter. We stood at the casket and cried, holding on to one another. We are descendants created at different times, belonging to different wombs, raised differently, yet by the same man. I know my father was pleased. This was the moment I had prayed so long for, this moment I had wished for and imagined time and again, had finally arrived. To be seen and acknowledged is a powerful thing. I was finally out of the shadows and standing in the light.

During the service, my father's nephew and great-niece sung a beautiful, moving selection, and everyone was standing to their feet, praising God. I was sitting in the second row, directly behind my father's wife, and at one point we were both standing up, praising and worshipping God. There is one God and both of us were praising Him at the same time. I couldn't help but wonder what her prayers to God all these years had been concerning her husband and their marriage. As a wife, you know, not praying for your spouse is like not praying for yourself. I assumed she had prayed and asked God to bless her husband and protect their marriage, along with many other things. Probably the same prayers I sent up for my husband. Were there times when God was receiving both of our prayers simultaneously? Hers for protection, mine for exposure? God is sovereign.

He does what He wants when He wants, and even when it doesn't seem like things are in order, they are.

Shortly after the benediction, she turned around to tell me that they were going to the cemetery. I couldn't quite hear her over the noise, but it sounded as if she was asking me if I was going to the cemetery. I went, and all of a sudden, I could tell by her body language she wasn't happy I was there. When we arrived at the cemetery I was seated by the funeral directors, directly up front.

After the last flower was placed on my father's casket, he was lowered into the ground, right next to Freshy. I got the chance to officially meet my brother, his wife, and a few of his children. I was ecstatic to meet my nieces and nephews. It turns out I have two great-nieces and two great-nephews. My brother sounds exactly like our father, and he has the same mannerisms. We exchanged contact info as I headed back to the church for the repass.

At the reception, my family and new cousins all sat down at my table, and I got to know them one by one. My father's daughter looked very much like she did that day she came to meet me when my father didn't want to go on the Oprah show. We only said a brief hello.

As the desserts were making their way around to the tables, my father's wife tapped me on the shoulder and asked if she could talk to me privately. I agreed and followed her through a hallway near the children's area of the church. We sat down by a window and she handed me a blue velour box with a bow on it. I opened it; it was a chain with a cross on it. She said it had belonged to my father and this was all she had for me. She emphasized that she was unsure why my father never spoke of me. She said something along the lines of she was led to believe that I didn't mean that much to him.

I had to take a few deep breaths. In my mind, I was saying, *No, he didn't tell you about me because he was going to have to explain that he was not only in my life but my mom's life as well.* I had to repeat to myself, *hold it together Heather. Hold it together. Don't fight hurt for hurt, it's the behavior of peasants. Don't do it.* She then continued to reiterate that my father must not have cared for me because he had given her specific instructions to take care of 'his girls', implying that he only cared for their daughter and granddaughter.

The rage I felt inside at that moment had my stomach in knots. I was mad at her, and I got mad at my father all over again, for not fixing this mess before he died.

I settled down by breathing and remembering I had forgiven my father. The epitome of forgiveness is letting go, not bringing it back up.

It was time for me to leave. I wasn't going to be her verbal punching bag. I realized her pain was deeper than the surface of the shade she was throwing. She wanted to hurt my mother, and by hurting me she knew she could hurt her. I wasn't going to give her the satisfaction of a frustrated frown. I smiled, and said, "My father and I had many ups and downs. He cared and provided for me for as long as I can remember. He paid for my college tuition and every car I drove. I assure you, I never wanted for anything." Then, I went a step further. "I knew my father's heart toward me, and up until the last day I saw him alive, he showered his love on me and his granddaughter."

I ended by saying, "God bless you," and we parted ways. As I got up, my father's cousin's daughter came to my rescue. We walked back to the table together, and I told Ron I was ready to go. He collected our belongings and I said goodbye to everyone I'd met.

Before we left, Ronney walked over to my father's wife, and said, "It was nice to meet you again." He knew I was hurt; he knew I had given her a pass, and he wanted her to hurt for hurting me. So, he thanked her for the furniture she and my father gave us a few weeks after we got married. The only thing is, she didn't know that furniture was given to me; I don't think she remembered that Ronney was the guy who came to pick up the furniture at their house. So petty! I had mixed emotions about him saying that to her, but then again, she asked for it. She chose to be mean.

CHAPTER TEN

Two years after my father's funeral, an investment company was trying to reach my father's wife regarding two properties Freshy owned in North Philadelphia—one of the properties being the one I lived in when I was little with my mom and sister. My father was the beneficiary of my grandmother's estate, and his wife told several people that she didn't want the properties. My father's cousin called me and told me to contact the investor. She felt, if anything, the properties should have gone to me.

After speaking with the investor, I mentioned that I would contact my siblings so that I wouldn't get into any legal trouble. When I spoke to my brother and sister, they were excited to work on this together. We were forming a relationship. My father's daughter had the properties assessed, and based on the lots in the area, both properties combined were worth hundreds of thousands of dollars. We talked things over amongst the three of us and agreed to find a realtor and sell the properties.

On February 17th, 2019, I received a call from my sister stating that her mother, my father's wife, had taken the properties back. She wanted to sell them exclusively. I found out she wasn't thrilled about the 'family reunion' between my siblings and me, so she took back what she initially didn't want. I admit I was pissed, but earlier that year, the Lord put in my spirit to write down thirty of His unconditional promises. When I wrote out those promises, I texted them to myself and saved them on my phone. It wasn't until I got that call that I read those promises repeatedly. I had reached my breaking point with this lady. I was ready to get in the car, drive to her home, knock on the door, and fight hurt with hurt.

I understand that I'm evidence of a vow that was broken. I'm a wife myself. I've done all I could to see this situation from her perspective, and as a wife I get where she is coming from. But has she ever once tried to do the same? Has she ever considered what it was like to be me growing up? Does she realize it wasn't me who betrayed her? I couldn't understand why she was robbing me of what belonged to me. More than that, I'm proof that God is sovereign, so she couldn't hate my existence yet love the creator. His word says, so.

After I went into prayer, God reminded me to reflect on those unconditional promises that didn't require me to do anything. I could be angry and bitter, and those promises still applied to me. I read them out loud, one by one. When I got to Isaiah 49:25, I stopped.

"But thus saith the Lord, Even the captives of the mighty shall be taken away, and the prey of the terrible shall be delivered: for I will contend with him that contendeth with thee and I will save thy children."

Wait a whole minute now, Jesus. I need you to CONTEND with her, because if I handle this, I will screw up immensely. Her taking back that real estate was personal, it was deliberate. This wasn't about her wanting the property. It was about my very existence; it was about revenge.

Every time I shifted my anger, Holy Spirit revealed that it was time to write the book, tell my story, and help someone else. It is time to turn my pain into purpose. I scrolled to another unconditional promise in Ezekiel, 36 verse 26 NKJV: "I will give you a new heart and put a new spirit within you; I will take the heart of stone out of your flesh and give you a heart of flesh."

Holy Spirit had said enough. The battle wasn't mine; it was never mine to fight from day one. The strategy was clear: heal, forgive, and help others. HEAL, FORGIVE, AND HELP OTHERS. Everything else is in His hands.

Months later, I saw online that the properties were sold. I was disappointed, but I remembered those promises and had faith that God was going to see to it that all would be handled. I published a journal of those Chosen Promises of God. It became an Amazon bestseller.

When I called my father's wife to ask her about the sale of the properties, she said she had lawyers involved. I said okay, and hung up. *God, what do you want me to do?* He didn't respond, so that meant be still.

In late October, I got a message on Ancestry.com that someone was interested in my grandmother's properties. I told them the properties had been sold. They wrote, "I have information that may help you, give me a call." I called, and they gave me credible information. I called an attorney, and before we got the paperwork started, I received a message from my father's wife's attorney, stating that the properties had actually been stolen... that they needed to be regained, and when they were properly sold, I would get my fair share.

According to New Jersey law, an illegitimate child is entitled to a percentage of their father's estate. Every state is different when it comes to children born out of wedlock, but in the state of New Jersey, I have rights and entitlements. Several months later I received a check for my legal percentage of the properties. It wasn't what I expected but it was a blessing, nonetheless. Inside the envelope was a letter apologizing for the delay. It was over. The perfect closure to a complicated journey.

Experiencing life as my father's secret, I look back now and realize there was a part of my father that was only trying to protect me, his wife, my mom, and himself. I was evidence of a vow broken; my existence had to remain a secret to prohibit pain. He did his best to protect us all from it. It turned out that pain was inevitable. I've learned that secrets are often kept because they are misunderstood. God forgave my father and so did I. When I hear stories from other people in similar situations, it turns out mine wasn't all that bad. And truth be told, it brought me closer to God. I have an endearing relationship with the Lord, and I trust Him with my entire life.

My best friend told me once that my spirit knew it was on an assignment long before it encompassed my body. God had a purpose to fulfill on earth, and my spirit said, "I'll do it!" My spirit wasn't going to sign up for a challenge it couldn't handle or win. So, when God says in His word, "I knew you before you were in your mother's womb," I believe He's speaking of my spirit. God knew exactly how I was going to come into this world. He knew my parents. He knew everything that I was going to experience as a secret child, and He knew one day, I'd write a book about it and change the search results on Google for 'children born in adultery'. My existence did not catch God off guard. Not at all. I leave you with these two things: forgive and focus.

FORGIVE

The more I put my trust in God, it became easier for me to forgive. I trust that He has a plan and that it's going to work in my favor. No matter the outcome, He's going to see to it that you are blessed.

I've learned that forgiveness is never for the person who hurt you. The act of forgiveness is for you. You forgive so that you are not carrying the weight of what someone else did to you. Forgive so that you can move forward. When you hold onto what someone did to you, it's like drinking poison and expecting someone else to die. Even if they are not sorry, forgive them. Before you leave this earth, you will do something that will require forgiveness. The bible tells us in Matthew chapter 18 verse 22, to forgive others seven times seventy. That's a lot.

First and foremost, forgive your parents. Your feelings are valid, and you have the right to be upset about how things are playing out in your life. Maybe you didn't have a fair beginning. Maybe you sometimes feel like you are getting the short end of the deal. All of this may be true, and still, I can't express enough that the key is to forgive. Forgive to set yourself free.

In fact, let's say a prayer of forgiveness:
Heavenly Father, I acknowledge that you are my creator. My existence did not take you by surprise. You already know the outcome before it ends. Unharden my heart so that I may forgive [insert name(s)]; they hurt me, and the pain is often unbearable. I confess that I forgive [insert name(s)] for [insert what they did to you]. In Matthew 6:14 your word says if I forgive those who sinned against me, you as my heavenly Father will forgive me.

Father God, not only do I forgive them, I ask that you bless them and, in your name, I pray, Amen.

AND FOCUS

There are over seven thousand promises in the bible from God to man. I have a journal of thirty unconditional promises of God. One unconditional promise that I hold dear to my heart is in Jeremiah chapter 29, verse 11:
"For I know the plans I have for you, declares the LORD, plans to prosper you and not to harm you, plans to give you hope and a future."

This promise says that the Lord has plans for you. Have you ever made plans? I'm a planner, and I take every detail into consideration. I'm human, yet God is supernatural, so just imagine the details He has planned for your life. He also says that the plans are for you to prosper. 'Prosper' means to succeed spiritually and in material terms; be financially successful, flourish physically, grow strong and healthy. That's the Oxford definition, but again, we serve a supernatural God, so 'to prosper' means that plus so much more.

His plan does not include harm. Nope. He does not want to harm us. In His word, Genesis 50:20 says that whatever harm comes our way, he'll turn it into good. He has plans to give us hope and a future. What a blessing. I could unwrap this verse a hundred ways, but I think you get it. No matter what your life looks like, no matter what you are experiencing, God has plans for you.

Focus on the promises of God, not the process. Jeremiah 29:11 is one scripture you must save to your phone, print it out and post it to your bathroom mirror and bedroom wall. Focus on that promise. You can apply it to just about every situation in your life. You already know the ending, YOU WIN!!!

I'd like to give you an opportunity to invite Christ into your heart if you do not know Him. Simply pray this prayer:
"Heavenly Father, I come to you in the mighty name of Jesus. Your Word says, "Whosoever shall call on the name of the Lord shall be saved." (Acts 2:21).

I am calling on you. I pray and ask Jesus to come into my heart and be Lord over my life according to Romans 10:9-10: "If thou shalt confess with thy mouth the Lord Jesus, and shalt believe in thine heart that God has raised Him from the dead, thou shalt be saved. For with the heart, man believeth unto righteousness, and with the mouth, confession is made unto salvation."

I confess that Jesus is Lord, and I believe in my heart that God raised Him from the dead. I am now reborn! I am a Christian—a child of Almighty God! I am saved! Amen.

I CHOOSE YOU

Heather James Miller

I don't want to blame the past for my neglect.
I didn't know who I was.
I didn't believe I was capable of giving love.
I chose others to love you instead.
Confident that they could give you more than what I had.

So, I chose "familiar love" that denied your existence; you just had to hide.

I chose "affectionate love," which came with danger; you just had to endure the risk of losing your life.

I chose "obsessive love," which came with bruises; you just had to keep quiet and turn a blind eye.

I chose "enduring love," which came with being second and unseen, your personality bottled up and kept comfortable on a shelf.

When I became whole, I realized I could love you myself, with "self-love," no stipulations, only deposits of wealth.

I love you with my whole being. I choose you, and you don't have to hide. It's not dangerous; it's full of life. No more bruises, no more intentional pain, this love sees you – all of you – mesmerized by your beauty and strength, this love is meant - I choose you.

ABOUT THE AUTHOR

Heather strongly believes that someone's traumatic past is someone else's present trauma. That theory inspired her to write the first book of the "Born In Adultery series, The Secret Daughter's Memoir," a personal testament of turning pain into purpose.

Heather created a bible study journal that features 30 Unconditional Promises of God. She confesses that in her Christian faith, her heart wasn't always in the right place; however, knowing that GOD made promises without prerequisites offered her confidence to triumph every obstacle in her life.

The journal made Amazon's Best Selling list for a week in 2019. The news attracted aspiring authors, and Heather consulted several of them on how to turn their traumatic testimonies into compelling books. Turning her 94 year old Grandmother Into an Amazon Best Selling Author.

When it comes to giving back, Heather advocates for children born in adultery. Her experience as a secret child endows parents and children of potential pain and hurdles they may face.Heather lives on the border of Northern Virginia's horse country with her family, and their Australian Labradoodle.

Made in the USA
Middletown, DE
22 March 2021

35467832R00068